Bulletproof Methods to Wealth Creation and Investing for Beginners:

Chapter 1: The Importance of Investing
- Why investing is crucial for building wealth.
- The benefits of investing over simply saving.
- Introducing the concept of compound interest.
- Building a solid financial foundation before investing.
- Creating an emergency fund.

Chapter 2: Understanding Investment Vehicles.
- Exploring different investment options: stocks, bonds, mutual funds, real estate, etc.
- Assessing the risks and potential returns of each investment vehicle
- The power of long-term investing in the stock market
- Harnessing the benefits of compounding
- Reinvesting dividends for long-term growth

Chapter 3: Diversification and Risk Management.
- The importance of diversifying your investment portfolio
- Spreading risk across different asset classes
- Ways to manage and mitigate investment risks
- The difference between investing for wealth and engaging in speculative trading
- Avoiding common pitfalls and risky investment behaviors

Chapter 4: Passive Investing and Index Funds
- Exploring the benefits of passive index funds and ETFs
- How to gain exposure to the stock market with lower fees and reduced risk
- The value of patience and a long-term mindset in investing
- Avoiding the pitfalls of trying to time the market or chase short-term gains

Chapter 5: Seeking Professional Advice
- The benefits of consulting with a financial advisor or investment professional
- Crafting an investment plan that aligns with your financial goals and risk tolerance
- The importance of staying informed about market trends and economic indicators

Chapter 6: Beating Inflation through Smart Investments
- Discussing the impact of inflation on the value of money
- Strategies for beating inflation by investing in solid and dependable vehicles such as Dividend King or Dividend Aristocrat stocks
- Importance of investing for retirement and leveraging time to build wealth
- Exploring various investment options including real estate, stocks, mutual funds, bonds, businesses, and precious metals for long-term financial security

Chapter 7: Achieving Early Retirement Through Investing.
- Exploring the concept of compound interest and its impact on wealth accumulation
- Understanding how compound interest can help generate wealth even after an economic depression
- The significance of protecting your principal while benefiting from compound interest
- The role of investing in securing a comfortable retirement.

Chapter 8: The power of compound interest
- How investing can make early retirement a realistic goal
- Transitioning from trading time for money to living off interest
- The feasibility of covering living expenses through investment returns
- Exploring the possibility of living off interest from investments
- Real-life examples of individuals who have achieved financial independence through investing

Chapter 9: Private Equity Investments for High-Net-Worth Individuals

High net worth individuals can take advantage of private equity investments made possible by sponsors that aren' t listed on the exchange.

Chapter 10: Trading Preferred Shares and Coupon Rates

Chapter 11: Securing Your Family's Future Through Smart Investing
- The role of smart investment choices in providing security for your family
- Creating investment accounts for children to leverage the power of compound interest
- Long-term financial planning for the benefit of future generations.

Chapter 12: Methods of Investing in Cryptocurrency
- **(1) Buying cryptocurrency directly**
  - Using cryptocurrency exchanges or broker-dealers
  - Commonly traded crypto coins

- **(2) Investing in cryptocurrency companies**
  - Indirect investment through shares of crypto-related firms
  - Types of companies involved in the crypto industry

- **(3) Investing in cryptocurrency-focused funds**
  - Indirect investment through funds tracking crypto asset performance
  - Types of funds: index funds, futures funds, investment trusts

- **(4) Investing in a cryptocurrency Roth IRA**
  - Specialized approach utilizing tax-advantaged retirement accounts
  - Utilizing a crypto IRA provider for account setup and management

Chapter 13: How can AI (Artificial Intelligence) assist in choosing right tools or better investment options for you?

Chapter 14: Principles of Wealth Growth and Investment
- Introduction to the principles of achievement in investing
- Emphasizing the importance of leaving invested money untouched to allow for growth
- Exploring methods to generate additional income through various entrepreneurial endeavors (selling merchandise, eBooks, blogging, etc.)
- Highlighting the value of seeking new ideas and opportunities for generating income

Chapter 15: Pursuing High Returns through Diversified Investments
- Comparing the returns of traditional savings accounts with other high-yield investment options
- Strategies for pursuing higher returns through a diversified investment portfolio.
- Exploring the concept of equity as a form of ownership in a company
- The potential for profits through equity investing and the risks involved
- Differentiating between individual stock investments, equity funds, and private equity investments

Chapter 16: Types of Fixed-Income Instruments
- Discussing various types of fixed-income instruments, such as certificates of deposit, treasury bonds, and preferred stock with stated dividend rates
- Providing examples of fixed-income investments and their potential returns over time
- Analyzing the suitability of fixed-income instruments for different investment objectives and risk profiles

Chapter 17: Attaining Financial Goals
- Emphasizing the possibility of retiring as a millionaire through disciplined investment and financial management
- Discussing the attainability of financial goals through disciplined investing
- Encouraging a simpler and more straightforward approach to investing.

Chapter 18: Wealth Building and Preservation
- Differentiating between wealth building and wealth preservation stages in life
- Addressing the diverse age range of individuals seeking financial guidance and the need for investments to reflect hard work and pay off

Bulletproof Methods to Wealth Creation and Investing for Beginners

Chapter 1: The Importance of Investing.

As we embark on the journey of financial empowerment, it's crucial to recognize the pivotal role that investing plays in building and securing wealth. Many people dream of financial independence, but without a solid understanding of the benefits of investing, such aspirations can remain elusive. In this chapter, we will delve into why investing is essential, the advantages it offers over simple saving, the power of compound interest, the importance of building a strong financial foundation, and the necessity of creating an emergency fund.

Why Investing is Crucial for Building Wealth:
Consider the story of two individuals, Alex and Taylor. Both have stable jobs and are diligent about saving money. Alex prefers to keep their savings in a traditional savings account, while Taylor decides to invest a portion of their savings in a diversified portfolio of stocks and bonds. Over time, despite both individuals saving the same amount, Taylor's invested funds grew significantly more than Alex's stagnant savings. This simple comparison illustrates the fundamental principle that investing has the potential to generate higher returns than traditional saving methods, ultimately accelerating the accumulation of wealth.

The Benefits of Investing Over Simply Saving:
Let's take a closer look at the benefits of investing over saving alone. When money is placed in a standard savings account, it typically earns minimal interest, often failing to outpace the rate of inflation. On the other hand, investing in various financial instruments such as stocks, bonds, mutual funds, or real estate presents the opportunity for substantial growth over the long term. Moreover, investing allows individuals to harness the power of various investment vehicles tailored to their risk tolerance and financial goals, thereby maximizing the potential for long-term prosperity.

Introducing the Concept of Compound Interest:
One of the most compelling reasons to invest is the concept of compound interest. Imagine a scenario where an individual invests a sum of money and earns interest not only on the initial investment but also on the accumulated interest from previous periods. Over time, this compounding effect can significantly boost the value of the investment, creating a snowball effect that accelerates wealth accumulation. To illustrate, consider an individual who starts investing in their 20s and consistently contributes to their investment portfolio. Due to the power of compounding, their investments have the potential to grow substantially by the time they reach retirement age, providing a comfortable financial cushion for their later years.

Building a Solid Financial Foundation Before Investing:
Before diving headfirst into the world of investing, it is vital to establish a robust financial foundation. This includes creating a budget to manage expenses, paying off high-interest debt, and ensuring adequate insurance coverage. By fortifying this financial groundwork, individuals can mitigate potential risks and lay the groundwork for a sustainable and successful investment strategy.

Creating an Emergency Fund:
An essential component of a secure financial foundation is the establishment of an emergency fund. Life is full of unexpected twists and turns and having a dedicated fund to cover unforeseen expenses such as medical emergencies, car repairs, or temporary unemployment provides a critical safety net. By setting aside three to six months' worth of living expenses in an accessible, low-risk account, individuals can navigate challenging times without jeopardizing their long-term financial plans.

Investing is a **skill.** It's perfectly possible to invest in something which increases in value but doesn't pay a *dividend.* To attain a great deal of *wealth,* your *money* must grow. For example, if you invest in a stock that does not pay a dividend, you're missing out on the **undeniable benefits** of **compound interest**.

From **forex trading** to **long-term investing, reinvesting dividend payments** is a fantastic way to grow your **funds.** If you know that **hard work** pays and you've been **brainstorming** on how to build greater wealth, you'll appreciate this book. Take advantage of these **financial instruments**; they are opportunities to create more wealth.

In conclusion, the decision to invest is a pivotal step toward securing a prosperous financial future. By understanding the benefits of investing over saving, harnessing the power of compound interest.

Chapter 2: Understanding Investment Vehicles.

Why should you invest?

As we venture deeper into the realm of investing, it becomes imperative to comprehend the diverse array of investment vehicles available to us. In this chapter, we will embark on a journey through various investment options—such as stocks, bonds, mutual funds, real estate, and more—assessing their inherent risks and potential returns. Additionally, we will uncover the profound influence of long-term investing in the stock market, and the compelling benefits derived from the phenomenon of compounding, including the strategic reinvestment of dividends for sustained growth.

Exploring Different Investment Options:
Stocks, Bonds, Mutual Funds, Real Estate—these are just a few of the numerous investment vehicles accessible to individuals seeking to expand their financial portfolios. Each of these options possesses unique characteristics and serves distinct investment objectives. For instance, stocks represent ownership in a company and offer the potential for significant capital appreciation, while bonds provide steady income through interest payments and are generally considered less volatile. Mutual funds, on the other hand, pool investors' money to invest in a diversified portfolio of assets, offering a convenient way to access a broad range of securities. Furthermore, real estate investments encompass a spectrum of opportunities, from residential properties to commercial ventures, presenting avenues for rental income and property appreciation.

Assessing Risks and Potential Returns:
Before engaging in any investment, it is imperative to conduct a comprehensive assessment of the associated risks and potential returns. Stocks, for example, are known for their volatility, as their value can fluctuate significantly in response to market conditions and company performance. Bonds, while generally offering more stability, are subject to interest rate risk and credit risk. Mutual funds carry their own set of risks, including market risk, manager risk, and fees. Real estate investments may be influenced by factors such as location, market demand, and property management. By thoroughly evaluating these factors, investors can make informed decisions aligned with their risk tolerance and financial goals.

The Power of Long-Term Investing in the Stock Market:
A fundamental principle of successful investing is the recognition of the power of long-term investment in the stock market. Despite short-term market fluctuations and occasional downturns, historical data consistently demonstrates the upward trajectory of the stock market over extended periods. By adopting a long-term perspective and remaining invested through market cycles, individuals can potentially benefit from the market's inclination to appreciate over time, thereby positioning themselves to capture substantial gains.

Harnessing the Benefits of Compounding:
At the core of successful investing lies the concept of compounding—the ability of an asset to generate earnings, which are then reinvested to generate their own earnings. Over time, this compounding effect can significantly amplify the growth of an investment. To illustrate, consider an individual who consistently reinvests the interest or dividends earned from their investments, allowing these earnings to generate additional returns. Through the magic of compounding, even modest initial investments have the potential to burgeon into substantial wealth over the course of several decades.

Reinvesting Dividends for Long-Term Growth:
Dividends, the distribution of a portion of a company's earnings to its shareholders, represent a compelling avenue for long-term growth. By reinvesting dividends back into

the underlying investment, individuals can acquire additional shares, thereby compounding their holdings and potentially accelerating wealth accumulation. This strategic approach not only augments the size of the investment, but also enhances the potential for future dividend payments.

In conclusion, you should invest if you plan to be wealthy or if you are wealthy and plan to keep it. **Saving** your wealth is only one part of the formula.

Your **savings** should be designated for investing purposes. Invest when the opportunity meets specific criteria, go beyond **speculation.**

At best, your **savings account** will grow at a **minimal rate**, perhaps 1% or 2%. How can be done in the event of an economic depression ***to make money after economic depression?*** You need to know how to make money after an economic depression. The **wealth that flows** in like an avalanche is the result of ***cash multiplying upon itself,*** made possible by investing.

Chapter 3: Diversification and Risk Management.

Top reasons to invest:

In the intricate landscape of investment, the principles of diversification and risk management stand as stalwart guardians of financial well-being. In this chapter, we will delve into the critical importance of diversifying investment portfolios, the art of spreading risk across different asset classes, strategies for managing and mitigating investment risks, the distinction between investing for wealth and engaging in speculative trading, and the imperative task of evading common pitfalls and risky investment behaviors.

The Importance of Diversifying Your Investment Portfolio:
Diversification serves as a cornerstone in the construction of a resilient investment portfolio. By spreading investments across various asset classes, industries, and geographic regions, individuals can reduce the impact of adverse events affecting any single investment or sector. For instance, during periods of economic downturn, certain sectors may experience declines while others remain resilient, thereby mitigating the overall impact on a diversified portfolio. Moreover, diversification allows investors to capture growth opportunities in multiple areas of the market, potentially enhancing long-term returns while mitigating portfolio volatility.

Spreading Risk Across Different Asset Classes:
The adage "don't put all your eggs in one basket" encapsulates the essence of spreading risk across different asset classes. By allocating investments across stocks,

bonds, real estate, and other instruments, individuals can create a balanced and resilient portfolio. In times of market turbulence, the performance of one asset class may offset losses in another, thereby safeguarding the overall value of the portfolio. Additionally, the inclusion of uncorrelated assets—those that tend to move independently of each other—further enhances diversification, as these assets may respond differently to market conditions.

Ways to Manage and Mitigate Investment Risks:
While no investment is entirely devoid of risk, prudent risk management strategies can help mitigate potential downsides. Techniques such as setting stop-loss orders to limit losses, conducting thorough due diligence before making investment decisions, and periodically rebalancing portfolios to maintain desired asset allocations can all contribute to effective risk management. Furthermore, the inclusion of defensive assets, such as high-quality bonds or cash equivalents, can provide stability during tumultuous market environments, acting as a buffer against volatility.

The Difference Between Investing for Wealth and Engaging in Speculative Trading:
A pivotal distinction in the realm of investment lies in the disparity between investing for wealth and engaging in speculative trading. Investing in wealth entails a disciplined, long-term approach focused on acquiring assets with the intent of generating sustainable growth and income over time. This approach often aligns with fundamental analysis and the assessment of a company's intrinsic value. Conversely, speculative trading involves short-term, high-risk endeavors driven by market speculation, momentum, or technical analysis. While speculative trading may yield rapid gains, it also carries heightened levels of risk and is often characterized by increased market volatility and uncertainty.

Avoiding Common Pitfalls and Risky Investment Behaviors:
In the pursuit of financial prosperity, it is imperative to sidestep common pitfalls and risky investment behaviors that can jeopardize long-term success. These may include succumbing to emotional decision-making, attempting to time the market, overconcentration in a single investment, or succumbing to "herd" mentality. Succumbing to herd mentality refers to the tendency for individuals to adopt the behaviors, beliefs, and opinions of the larger group, or "herd," rather than making independent decisions. When people succumb to herd mentality, they may abandon their own critical thinking and instead conform to the prevailing attitudes or actions of the group. By maintaining a disciplined, objective approach to investing, grounded in comprehensive research and a long-term perspective, individuals can fortify their financial positions and navigate the complexities of the investment landscape with prudence and confidence.

In conclusion, Investing allows you to **protect your principal** while _**generating compound interest**_. Compound interest is one of the most powerful forces on Earth, making it possible to make money after an **economic depression** how to make money after economic depression. As important as it is to grow your money, it is equally important to make sure your **initial investment** doesn't go anywhere.

Investing gives you the assurance that you can **retire and thrive rather than survive.** It provides you with **a solid way to earn income while protecting the money you've labored to earn**. A few simple calculations will show you how much money you need to **invest and at what interest rate to be financially free for retirement.** Investing makes early retirement possible.

Chapter 4: Passive Investing and Index Funds.

In the dynamic realm of investment, the concept of passive investing and the utilization of index funds and exchange-traded funds (ETFs) have emerged as compelling avenues for individuals seeking to access the stock market with prudence and efficiency. In this chapter, we will illuminate the benefits of passive index funds and ETFs, elucidate the methods to gain exposure to the stock market with lower fees and reduced risk, underscore the value of patience and a long-term mindset in investing, and caution against the perilous pitfalls of attempting to time the market or pursue short-term gains.

Exploring the Benefits of Passive Index Funds and ETFs:

Passive index funds and ETFs have garnered widespread recognition for their ability to provide broad market exposure at a relatively low cost. These investment vehicles, which aim to replicate the performance of a specific market index, offer investors the opportunity to participate in the growth of the overall market without the burden of attempting to pick individual stocks. Furthermore, passive index funds and ETFs generally feature lower management fees compared to actively managed funds, making them an attractive option for cost-conscious investors seeking to maximize their investment returns.

How to Gain Exposure to the Stock Market with Lower Fees and Reduced Risk:

By channeling investments into passive index funds and ETFs, individuals can attain diversified exposure to the stock market while mitigating specific risks associated with individual stock selection. Rather than assuming the burden of researching, analyzing, and selecting individual stocks, investors can harness the collective performance of a broad market index, such as the S&P 500 or the total stock market index. Additionally, the lower fees associated with passive index funds and ETFs contribute to a more efficient allocation of investment capital, potentially enhancing long-term returns by minimizing the impact of fees on overall performance.

The Value of Patience and a Long-Term Mindset in Investing:

At the heart of passive investing lies the value of patience and a steadfast long-term mindset. Instead of succumbing to the allure of short-term market fluctuations or attempting to time the market, passive investors embrace the enduring philosophy of remaining invested through market cycles. By adopting a patient and disciplined approach, individuals can position themselves to capture the inherent growth of the market over extended periods, thus potentially reaping the rewards of long-term wealth accumulation.

Avoiding the Pitfalls of Trying to Time the Market or Chase Short-Term Gains:
A cardinal rule in passive investing is the avoidance of attempting to time the market or chase short-term gains. Market timing, the act of buying and selling assets based on predictions of market movements, often proves to be a perilous endeavor, as accurately forecasting market fluctuations with consistency is exceedingly challenging. In a similar vein, the pursuit of short-term gains can lead to impulsive decision-making and heightened levels of risk. By focusing on a long-term investment horizon and adhering to a disciplined, passive strategy, individuals can cultivate a stable and sustainable approach to wealth accumulation, insulated from the volatility and uncertainties of short-term market movements.

By embracing the principles of passive investing and index funds, individuals can position themselves to access the stock market efficiently, minimize fees, and cultivate a prudent, long-term investment strategy grounded in patience and resilience.

In conclusion, Ideally, you want to **stop trading your time for money and have your expenses paid for by interest**. Living from interest is possible, and investors have found ways to cover many of their costs this way, if not all of them.

While you may think that wealth is an astronomical number, **the effects of wealth can certainly be felt when bills can be paid with dividend payments**.

Provide a higher level of security for your family by **making smart investment choices with your money**. If there are small children in your family, time is on your side. **You can open an account for them with a healthy interest rate and let the**

compound interest builds into their adulthood.

Chapter 5: Seeking Professional Advice.

Facilitate a way for your money to grow:

As we navigate the complex and ever-evolving landscape of investment, the wisdom of seeking professional advice from a financial advisor or investment professional emerges as a pivotal strategy in the pursuit of financial well-being. In this chapter, we will illuminate the benefits of consulting with a financial advisor, elucidate the process of crafting an investment plan that aligns with financial goals and risk tolerance, and underscore the importance of staying informed about market trends and economic indicators.

The Benefits of Consulting with a Financial Advisor or Investment Professional:

Engaging the services of a seasoned financial advisor or investment professional can yield a myriad of benefits for individuals seeking to fortify their financial positions. These professionals bring a wealth of expertise and insights, offering tailored guidance and recommendations aligned with an individual's unique financial circumstances and aspirations. By leveraging their knowledge of investment strategies, tax implications, retirement planning, and risk management, individuals can gain a comprehensive understanding of their financial options and make informed decisions that resonate with their long-term goals.

Crafting an Investment Plan Aligned with Financial Goals and Risk Tolerance:

A foundational aspect of seeking professional advice involves crafting a well-defined investment plan that harmonizes with an individual's financial goals and risk tolerance. Through collaborative discussions with a financial advisor, individuals can articulate their aspirations, whether they pertain to retirement planning, wealth accumulation, or legacy building. Furthermore, a thorough assessment of risk tolerance, liquidity needs, and time horizon enables the formulation of an investment strategy tailored to navigate market fluctuations while remaining aligned with an individual's comfort level and objectives.

The Importance of Staying Informed about Market Trends and Economic Indicators:

While enlisting the expertise of a financial advisor is invaluable, it is also essential for individuals to cultivate a foundational understanding of market trends and economic indicators. By staying informed about macroeconomic factors, industry developments, and geopolitical events, individuals can contextualize the advice received from their financial advisors and make well-informed decisions. Moreover, a nuanced awareness of market dynamics empowers individuals to actively engage in discussions with their advisors, fostering a collaborative and informed approach to managing their investment portfolios.

In conclusion, seeking professional advice from a financial advisor or investment professional serves as an indispensable ally in the journey toward financial prosperity. By harnessing their expertise, individuals can craft investment plans tailored to their unique financial circumstances, aspirations, and risk tolerance, while also cultivating a foundational understanding of market trends and economic indicators. This collaborative approach equips individuals with the knowledge and confidence to navigate the complexities of the investment landscape and make informed decisions that resonate with their long-term financial objectives.

<u>Chapter 6: Beating Inflation through Smart Investments.</u>

In the previous chapters, we've delved into the fundamental principles of wealth creation
and investing. Now, let's take a closer look at real-life examples of successful
investment strategies employed by individuals who have achieved financial success
through prudent and strategic investment decisions.

<u>1. The Power of Compound Interest in Action:</u>

- Sarah's Story: Sarah started investing $200 per month in a low-cost index fund at the
age of 25. By consistently contributing to her investment portfolio and harnessing the
power of compound interest, she accumulated a substantial nest egg by the time she
reached 50, allowing her to retire comfortably and pursue her passions.

<u>2. Diversification and Risk Management in a Volatile Market:</u>

- John and Lisa's Portfolio: John and Lisa diversified their investment portfolio across
various asset classes, including stocks, bonds, real estate, and commodities. During
periods of market volatility, their diversified holdings helped mitigate risk and preserve
capital, providing them with stability and consistent returns over the long term.

<u>3. Investing for the Long Term: Weathering Market Fluctuations:</u>

- Michael's Experience: Michael remained steadfast in his commitment to long-term
investing, ignoring short-term market fluctuations and focusing on the underlying
strength of his investment choices. This patient approach allowed him to weather
market downturns and benefit from the compounding effect of his investments,
ultimately achieving significant growth and financial security.

<u>4. Passive Investing and Index Funds: A Strategy for Sustainable Growth:</u>

- Emily's Journey: Emily opted for passive index funds and exchange-traded funds
(ETFs) to gain exposure to the stock market while minimizing fees and reducing risk. By
maintaining a long-term perspective and avoiding the temptation to engage in
speculative trading, she steadily built wealth and secured her financial future.

<u>5. Professional Guidance and Tailored Investment Plans:</u>

- Mark's Success: Mark sought the expertise of a financial advisor to craft a
personalized investment plan aligned with his financial goals and risk tolerance. With
the guidance of his advisor, Mark constructed a well-diversified portfolio and navigated
market uncertainties with confidence, achieving steady growth and financial prosperity.

By examining these real-life examples, we gain valuable insights into the practical
application of wealth creation and investment principles. These success stories
underscore the significance of disciplined investing, prudent risk management, and the
long-term perspective in building lasting wealth. As we continue our journey toward

financial empowerment, these examples serve as inspirations for our own investment endeavors, guiding us toward a prosperous and secure financial future.

In conclusion, **Beat inflation**

Unfortunately, due to inflation, the value of money decreases. **You don' t have to let inflation have an adverse effect on your financial future**.

Beat inflation by placing your money in **solid investment vehicles that are dependable**, such as a **Dividend King or a Dividend Aristocrat**.

Chapter 7: Achieving Early Retirement Through Investing.
Invest for retirement:

As you start to explore the concept of achieving early retirement through investing, it's essential to understand the powerful impact of compound interest on wealth accumulation. Compound interest is the addition of interest to the principal sum of a loan or deposit, or in other words, it's interest on interest. This means that not only does your initial investment grow, but the growth itself generates even more growth over time.

Consider the following example: Suppose you invest $10,000 in a retirement account at an annual interest rate of 7%. In the first year, you would earn $700 in interest, bringing the total to $10,700. In the second year, you would earn $749 in interest, bringing the total to $11,449, and so on. Over time, the growth curve becomes steeper, and the power of compounding becomes increasingly evident.

Furthermore, understanding how compound interest can help generate wealth even after an economic depression is crucial. While economic downturns can be unsettling, a well-diversified investment portfolio with a focus on long-term growth can weather the storm. History has shown that, despite market fluctuations, a disciplined approach to investing has allowed many individuals to preserve and grow their wealth over time.

Protecting your principal while benefiting from compound interest is another key consideration. By investing in a mix of assets such as stocks, bonds, and real estate, you can mitigate risk while still taking advantage of the compounding effect. Diversification can help cushion your portfolio from the impact of market volatility, ensuring that your principal is safeguarded while your investments continue to grow.

When it comes to securing a comfortable retirement, the role of investing cannot be overstated. By diligently contributing to retirement accounts such as 401(k)s, IRAs, or other investment vehicles, you can harness the power of compound interest to build a substantial nest egg. This, coupled with strategic asset allocation and regular rebalancing, can set you on the path to financial independence and an early retirement that aligns with your aspirations.

In conclusion, understanding the concepts of compound interest and its role in retirement investing is fundamental to achieving financial freedom. By harnessing the potential of compounding, protecting your principal, and making informed investment decisions, you can pave the way for a secure and prosperous retirement.

By investing now and taking advantage of time, you can hold **real estate**, **stocks**, **mutual funds**, **bonds,** **businesses**, and **precious metals for many years**.

You can **spread your money across these investments** according to your risk tolerance to have a stable way to grow wealth and retire comfortably.

By having high long-term return than a savings account, you' re more likely to hold the funds over the long-term. **Keeping your money and allowing it to grow** helps you make major purchases such as a **home**, **car**, **college,** or **investment in your own business.**

Investment vehicles offer different tax opportunities. For example, you can **lower your taxable income by taking pre-tax money and investing it into a 401k or other retirement fund.**

Typical **savings accounts** at a bank or credit union are no match for other investments with a much higher yield.

Chapter 8: The Power of Compound Interest

As you delve into the world of personal finance and investing, you'll soon realize that achieving early retirement is not merely a dream but a realistic goal, thanks to the extraordinary power of compound interest. In this chapter, we will explore how investing can transform the traditional notion of trading time for money into the liberating concept of living off interest and investment returns.

Making Early Retirement Attainable:

By harnessing the potential of compound interest through strategic investment, individuals can transform their financial outlook and make early retirement a tangible objective. Through disciplined saving and prudent investment choices, it's possible to build a robust portfolio that generates substantial returns over time, ultimately paving the way for a retirement that is not tethered to a traditional work schedule.

Transitioning to Living Off Interest:

Shifting from the paradigm of trading time for money to living off interest marks a fundamental transition in one's financial journey. As your investments grow and compound, the income generated from interest and dividends can gradually replace the need for active employment income. This shift empowers individuals to embrace a lifestyle driven by personal passions and pursuits rather than the necessity of a paycheck.

Feasibility of Covering Living Expenses:
One of the most compelling aspects of retirement through investing is the prospect of covering living expenses through sustainable investment returns. With a well-structured investment portfolio and a focus on income-generating assets, individuals can create a reliable stream of cash flow that supports their desired standard of living, thus providing the financial freedom to pursue their interests and aspirations.

Living Off Interest: A Viable Reality:
The concept of living off interest from investments is not merely theoretical; it is a tangible reality for many individuals who have diligently built and managed their investment portfolios. By focusing on assets that produce consistent income, such as dividend-paying stocks, bonds, and real estate, it is indeed feasible to sustain a fulfilling lifestyle through the interest and returns generated by these investments.

Real-Life Examples of Financial Independence:
To provide further insight into the potential of achieving financial independence through investing, we will explore real-life examples of individuals who have successfully navigated the path to early retirement. Through prudent financial planning, strategic investment decisions, and a commitment to long-term wealth accumulation, these individuals have realized their dreams of financial independence and are now enjoying the rewards of their foresight and dedication.

In conclusion, the power of compound interest and the potential of investing offer a transformative pathway to early retirement and financial independence. By embracing these concepts, individuals can embark on a journey toward a future that is defined by personal fulfillment, autonomy, and the realization of lifelong aspirations.

If you want more returns than your savings account can give you, it's time to **find an investment vehicle with the appropriate yield and risk to meet your financial goals.**

Equity is a portion of ownership in the company and the right to profits the company earns in the future. **Equity investing** consists of **buying shares or stocks and the interest generated on those shares.**

These investments might be considered **high risk, high reward**. With equity investments, the money you put in is only recovered when you **sell your shareholdings** or if the **firm liquidates and distributes proceeds.**

In general, assets minus liabilities equal the company' s equity. **Equity is ownership** once all debts have been subtracted. **Financial sponsors are private equity investment firms** that invest in **private companies** to create demand.

You can buy private equity investments funded by sponsors, individual stocks, or equity funds.

Chapter 9: Private Equity Investments for High-Net-Worth Individuals.

For high-net-worth individuals seeking to diversify their investment portfolios and access exclusive opportunities, private equity investments present a compelling avenue for wealth creation and strategic asset allocation. Unlike publicly traded securities, private equity investments offer a distinct realm of investment possibilities that are not readily available to the public. In this chapter, we will explore the unique landscape of private equity investments and the potential benefits they hold for high-net-worth individuals.

Accessing Exclusive Opportunities:

Private equity investments provide high-net-worth individuals with access to a range of investment opportunities that are not available through publicly traded markets. These investments are often made in private companies, start-ups, real estate ventures, and other non-publicly traded assets, enabling investors to participate in ventures that may have significant growth potential and offer attractive returns.

Beyond Publicly Listed Securities:

Unlike traditional stocks and bonds that are listed on public exchanges, private equity investments are not subject to the same level of regulatory oversight and are not readily accessible to the general investing public. This exclusivity allows high-net-worth individuals to engage in opportunities that are often shielded from the volatility and short-term pressures of public markets, thus providing a distinct avenue for long-term wealth creation.

Strategic Partnership with Sponsors:

High-net-worth individuals can forge strategic partnerships with private equity sponsors, who serve as the driving force behind these non-public investments. These sponsors, often comprising experienced investment professionals and industry experts, bring forth a wealth of knowledge and resources to identify, evaluate, and manage private equity opportunities, thereby offering investors the potential to capitalize on specialized market insights and expertise.

Diverse Investment Vehicles:

Private equity investments encompass a diverse range of vehicles, including venture capital funds, private equity funds, real estate funds, and direct investments in private companies. This diversity allows high-net-worth individuals to tailor their investment strategies to align with their risk tolerance, investment horizon, and sector-specific preferences, thereby creating a bespoke approach to wealth management and growth.

<u>**Risk and Reward Dynamics:**</u>
While private equity investments can offer the potential for substantial returns, it's important to recognize that they also carry inherent risks, including illiquidity, lack of transparency, and longer investment horizons. High-net-worth individuals must carefully evaluate these factors and consider the potential trade-offs in pursuit of the unique growth opportunities presented by private equity investments.

In conclusion, private equity investments present an intriguing landscape for high-net-worth individuals seeking to expand their investment horizons and capitalize on exclusive opportunities. By engaging in private equity investments, these individuals can access a diverse range of investment prospects, leverage the expertise of experienced sponsors, and potentially unlock significant value beyond the scope of traditional publicly traded securities, thereby enriching their investment strategies and fostering long-term wealth creation.

High net worth individuals can take advantage of private equity investments made possible by sponsors that aren't listed on the exchange.

The benefit of investing in costly private equity investments is the substantial portion of ownership investors walk away with.

With **fixed-income securities**, you receive a return through **periodic payments that eventually return the principal**. Once the security reaches maturity, the **principle is returned to you.** The payments remain the same for the life of the security and are known to you in advance.

The principal is returned to you through either a **dividend on preferred stock**, **coupon payment, or interest payment.**

Fixed income securities typically have a **lower rate of return than variable-income security.** This type of investment is appropriate for investors averse to risk. There are different **types of fixed-income instruments including** *certificates of deposit*, *treasury bonds*, and a *preferred stock with a stated dividend* rate. For example, if you buy a 30-year security for $1,000 with a 4% interest rate, this investment will pay you $40 annually for the next 30 years. At the end of the 30 years, the $1,000 principal is returned to you.

Chapter 10: Trading Preferred Shares and Coupon Rates

Preferred shares

As investors seek to diversify their portfolios and explore avenues for income generation, trading preferred shares and understanding coupon rates can provide a distinctive opportunity to navigate the complexities of the financial markets. In this chapter, we will delve into the realm of preferred shares and coupon rates, examining their significance in trading and the considerations that underpin these investment instruments.

Understanding Preferred Shares:

Preferred shares represent a unique class of equity ownership in a company, offering investors a hybrid security that combines elements of both stocks and bonds. Unlike common shares, preferred shares typically entitle their holders to fixed dividends, priority in receiving assets in the event of liquidation, and, in some cases, the potential for capital appreciation. By delving into the world of preferred shares, investors can gain exposure to a diverse array of companies and industries while potentially benefiting from steady income streams.

Exploring Coupon Rates:

The coupon rate of a preferred share, or any fixed-income security, represents the annual interest rate paid out as a percentage of the face value of the security. Understanding coupon rates is essential for investors aiming to gauge the income potential and relative attractiveness of preferred shares within their investment portfolios. By analyzing the coupon rates of preferred shares, investors can assess the yield on their investment, compare it to alternative fixed-income securities, and make informed decisions regarding income generation and capital preservation.

Trading Dynamics and Liquidity Considerations:

When trading preferred shares, investors should consider the dynamics of the market and the liquidity of the securities. While preferred shares may offer attractive dividend yields and potential tax advantages, they often exhibit lower liquidity compared to common stocks. Understanding the trading dynamics and liquidity considerations associated with preferred shares is crucial for investors seeking to make informed decisions and effectively navigate the market for these unique investment instruments.

Risk and Return Profiles:

Assessing the risk and return profiles of preferred shares is paramount for investors, as these securities encompass a spectrum of risk levels and income potential. By evaluating factors such as credit quality, interest rate environments, and company-specific considerations, investors can gain insights into the risk-adjusted return potential of preferred shares and align their investment strategies with their financial objectives and risk tolerance.

<u>**Tax Implications and Diversification Strategies:**</u>
Investors trading preferred shares should also consider the tax implications of receiving dividends and interest income, as well as the potential advantages of diversifying their portfolios through exposure to various sectors and issuers. Understanding the interplay between tax considerations and diversification strategies is essential for optimizing the income and growth potential of preferred shares within a comprehensive investment framework.

In conclusion, trading preferred shares and understanding coupon rates represent a nuanced dimension of investment strategy, offering investors the potential for income generation, capital preservation, and portfolio diversification. By delving into the intricacies of preferred shares and coupon rates, investors can expand their investment horizons, leverage the income potential of fixed-income securities, and tailor their portfolios to align with their financial goals and risk preferences.

Preferred shares have a **greater claim on a corporation' s assets than common stock**.

Preferred shares usually pay a dividend that does not include **voting rights**. **Dividends are paid to preferred shareholders before common stock**.

Preferred shares provide a **higher level of protection for the shareholder** because they are entitled to **assets** should the **company become insolvent**.

You can buy and sell preferred shares through an **online broker**. These shares are typically not as **volatile as common shares.**

The interest rate you' ll be paid is known as the **coupon rate**. Although, you may have a rate that "floats" based upon **Libor (the international benchmark rate).** If a company suspends dividends, the **cumulative preferred stock continues** to accrue and is paid to the investor after the suspension ends.

Non-cumulative preferred stock dividends are gone forever if the company suspends issuing dividends. Of course, a company suspending its dividends is a sign of **financial**

distress. Preferred share dividends are released quarterly and, in some cases, monthly. Since this investment type has no **maturity date,** they are **perpetual.**

With mutual funds, money is pooled together from investors and then invested in **securities** in the form of **short-term debt, bonds,** and **stocks**. All the holdings within a mutual fund are referred to as its **portfolio**.

Mutual funds provide the opportunity to invest in hundreds or even thousands of **individual securities**. There are **no-load mutual funds** that reduce costs by charging a **single expense ratio rather than accruing commissions** from selling and buying by yourself. Mutual funds do not include voting rights as stocks do.

Chapter 11: Securing Your Family's Future Through Smart Investing.

In the pursuit of securing your family's future, smart investment choices play a pivotal role in laying the foundation for financial stability, growth, and the realization of multi-generational aspirations. This chapter will explore the significance of smart investing in providing security for your family, the potential of creating investment accounts for children to harness the power of compound interest, and the enduring impact of long-term financial planning for the benefit of future generations.

Empowering Financial Security through Smart Investments:

Smart investment choices are instrumental in safeguarding the financial well-being of your family and establishing a legacy of resilience and prosperity. By strategically allocating resources across diverse investment vehicles, such as stocks, bonds, real estate, and other assets, families can fortify their financial positions, mitigate risk, and lay the groundwork for sustained wealth accumulation and protection.

Leveraging the Power of Compound Interest for Children:

Creating investment accounts for children represents a powerful strategy for leveraging the inherent strength of compound interest and nurturing a culture of financial literacy and responsibility from an early age. By establishing avenues for long-term growth, such as custodial accounts, 529 college savings plans, or dedicated investment portfolios, families can provide their children with a financial head start and the opportunity to capitalize on the compounding effect to secure their own future financial independence.

Long-Term Financial Planning for Future Generations:

Embracing a holistic approach to long-term financial planning is essential for safeguarding the prosperity of future generations within the family. By formulating comprehensive estate plans, establishing trusts, and implementing intergenerational wealth transfer strategies, families can ensure the seamless preservation and transmission of assets, values, and opportunities, thereby leaving a lasting and meaningful legacy for their descendants.

<u>**Education and Empowerment:**</u>
Beyond financial considerations, smart investing also encompasses the education and empowerment of family members to make informed financial decisions and cultivate a shared understanding of the family's wealth management strategies. By fostering open communication, providing financial education, and instilling a sense of stewardship, families can nurture a culture of responsible wealth management and equip future generations with the knowledge and tools to uphold and expand the family's financial legacy.

<u>**Environmental, Social, and Governance (ESG) Considerations:**</u>
In the spirit of securing the family's future, families can also integrate environmental, social, and governance (ESG) considerations into their investment strategies, aligning their financial endeavors with broader societal and ethical objectives. By investing in companies and initiatives that prioritize sustainability, social responsibility, and ethical governance, families can contribute to a more equitable and sustainable future while concurrently securing their family's financial interests.

In conclusion, securing your family's future through smart investing transcends mere financial considerations and encompasses a profound commitment to resilience, empowerment, and intergenerational prosperity. By embracing smart investment choices, nurturing the potential of compound interest for children, and engaging in long-term financial planning, families can fortify their legacies and pave the way for enduring financial security, growth, and fulfillment across generations.

One way to earn a return is through the <u>**distribution of dividends**</u>-you can either get a <u>**check or reinvest the earnings**</u>.

Mutual funds are required to pass all <u>**net income to shareholders**</u>; this allows the fund to avoid paying earnings taxes. The payment schedule of this investment varies. Payments are made either annually, monthly, or quarterly.

The *second way* mutual funds generate income is through <u>**selling securities with increased price because of capital gain**</u>. You can also make gains from foreign <u>**exchange**</u>; it's treated as a <u>**capital gain if the gain is greater than $200**</u>.

If the fund's holdings increase in price, the shares do too. Favorable breaks may cause your shares to increase in price, allowing you to sell the mutual funds at a profit.

Derivatives derive their value from something else. It is not the derivative itself that is valuable, but what the derivative represents. Nearly anything can form the underlying basis of a **derivative contract**.

Forwards are defined as a **customized contract** between two parties to sell or buy an asset at a certain price on a specified future date.

Futures are like forwards but are **regulated and standardized.** A future track the prices of the underlying asset without you needing to own the underlying asset. For example, you wouldn't need to store grain or aluminum yourself.

An **option** is a contract that allows you to have the right to sell or buy a financial asset without an obligation to do so.

Options give you a choice to call or put, making this investment option a bit more flexible than a future. If you buy a call, you want the stock to go up. If you buy a putt, you want the stock to go down. The longer you have an option, the more you must pay. Think of options such as insurance that you pay for monthly.

Swaps are a simple exchange of securities. With a swap, the interest rate, **cash flow**, or **liability is exchanged between two parties through a derivative contract**. You won't find swaps traded on exchanges.

Chapter 12: Methods of Investing in Cryptocurrency

INVESTING IN CRYPTOCURRENCY:

Investing in cryptocurrency is a popular and exciting way to diversify your portfolio, but it also involves some risks and challenges. There are different ways to invest in crypto, depending on your goals, preferences, and level of expertise. Here are some of the most common methods:

(1) Buying cryptocurrency directly:

This is the simplest and most direct way to invest in crypto. You can use a cryptocurrency exchange or a broker-dealer to buy and sell crypto coins, such as Bitcoin, Ethereum, Litecoin, and many others. You will need a digital wallet to store your coins, which can be either online, offline, or hardware based. Some of the advantages of buying crypto directly are that you have full control over your coins, you can benefit from price appreciation, and you can use your coins for transactions or transfers. Some of the disadvantages are that you must deal with security issues, transaction fees, volatility, and regulatory uncertainty.

(2) Investing in cryptocurrency companies:

This is a more indirect way to invest in crypto, by buying shares of companies that are involved in the crypto industry. These can be companies that mine crypto, produce mining hardware, support crypto transactions, hold crypto on their balance sheets, or offer other crypto-related services. Some of the advantages of investing in crypto companies are that you can access the crypto market through traditional stock platforms, you can diversify your exposure, and you can benefit from the growth potential of the crypto industry. Some of the disadvantages are that you must pay commissions and taxes, you are subject to market risk, and you may not capture the full upside of crypto price movements.

(3) Investing in cryptocurrency-focused funds:

This is another indirect way to invest in crypto, by buying shares of funds that track the performance of crypto assets, such as index funds, futures funds, or investment trusts. These funds can offer exposure to a single crypto coin, a basket of coins, or a crypto-related sector.

Some of the advantages of investing in crypto funds are that you can access the crypto market through regulated and liquid vehicles, you can diversify your portfolio, and you can benefit from professional management. Some of the disadvantages are that you must pay fees and expenses, you may face tracking errors or liquidity issues, and you may not have direct ownership of the underlying coins.

(4) Investing in a cryptocurrency Roth IRA:

This is a special way to invest in crypto, by using a tax-advantage retirement account that allows you to buy and sell crypto coins. You can use a crypto IRA provider to set up and manage your account, which can offer more security and convenience than a regular crypto exchange or wallet.

Some of the advantages of investing in a crypto Roth IRA are that you can enjoy tax-free growth and withdrawals, you can diversify your retirement savings, and you can avoid early withdrawal penalties. Some of the disadvantages are that you must pay fees and commissions, you are subject to contribution limits and distribution rules, and you may face regulatory uncertainty.

As you can see, there are many ways to invest in crypto, each with its own pros and cons. Before you decide which method suits you best, you should do your own research, understand the risks, and consult a financial professional if needed. Investing in crypto can be rewarding, but also challenging, so make sure you are prepared and informed.

Chapter 13: How can AI (Artificial Intelligence) assist in choosing right tools or better investment options for you?

AI can assist individuals in making investment decisions and choosing the right investment tools or options in several ways:

1. Data Analysis: AI can analyze vast amounts of financial data from various sources to identify patterns, trends, and potential investment opportunities. By processing and interpreting this data, AI can provide insights into market conditions, asset performance, and risk factors, helping individuals make informed investment decisions.

2. Risk Assessment: AI-powered tools can assess the risk associated with different investment options by analyzing historical data, market volatility, and other relevant factors. This can help individuals understand the potential risks and rewards of specific investments and make more calculated decisions.

3. Portfolio Optimization: AI algorithms can help optimize investment portfolios by recommending asset allocations based on an individual's financial goals, risk tolerance, and investment horizon. By considering a wide range of investment options, AI can suggest diversified portfolios that align with an individual's preferences and objectives.

4. Personalized Recommendations: AI-driven platforms can provide personalized investment recommendations based on an individual's financial profile, investment preferences, and long-term goals. These recommendations can help individuals discover investment options that are tailored to their specific needs and circumstances.

5. Market Insights: AI-powered tools can provide real-time market insights and news, helping individuals stay informed about market developments, economic indicators, and industry trends that may impact investment decisions.

6. Behavioral Analysis: AI can analyze an individual's investment behavior and decision-making patterns to provide personalized feedback and insights. By understanding an individual's biases and tendencies, AI can help mitigate emotional decision-making and encourage more rational investment choices.

7. Automation and Robo-Advisors: AI-driven robot-advisors can automate investment processes, such as asset allocation, rebalancing, and tax optimization, based on predefined criteria and individual preferences. This can help individuals manage their investments efficiently and cost-effectively.

Overall, AI can be a valuable resource for individuals seeking to invest, offering data-driven insights, personalized recommendations, and automation to support informed decision-making and help individuals navigate the complexities of the investment landscape.

Chapter 14: Principles of Wealth Growth and Investment

Principles of achievement

As we delve into the principles of wealth growth and investment, it's essential to lay the groundwork for understanding the key factors that contribute to successful financial endeavors. In this chapter, we will explore the fundamental principles of achieving success in investing, emphasizing the importance of leaving invested money untouched to allow for organic growth. Additionally, we'll discuss methods to generate additional income through various entrepreneurial endeavors, such as selling merchandise, creating eBooks, and engaging in blogging. Finally, we will underline the value of seeking new ideas and opportunities for generating income, thus paving the way for a prosperous financial future.

Leaving Money Invested for Growth:

One of the fundamental principles of wealth growth is the understanding that investments require time to yield substantial returns. By leaving money invested in sound financial instruments such as stocks, mutual funds, or real estate, individuals can benefit from compounding interest and market appreciation. For instance, let's consider the case of an individual who invests in a diversified portfolio of stocks and reinvests the dividends earned. Over time, the initial investment has the potential to grow significantly, showcasing the power of patience and long-term vision in wealth accumulation.

Generating Additional Income through Entrepreneurial Endeavors:
In today's interconnected world, there are countless opportunities to generate additional income through entrepreneurial pursuits. Whether it's establishing an online store to sell merchandise, writing and publishing eBooks, or creating engaging content through blogging, individuals have the chance to leverage their skills and passions into profitable ventures. For example, an individual with a flair for crafting may decide to set up an e-commerce store to sell handmade products, tapping into a global market and diversifying their income streams.

Seeking New Ideas and Opportunities for Income Generation:
In the quest for financial prosperity, the value of seeking new ideas and opportunities cannot be overstated. This may involve staying abreast of market trends, networking with like-minded individuals, or actively seeking out potential investment avenues. For instance, an individual passionate about sustainable living may identify a burgeoning market for eco-friendly products and decide to explore the possibility of launching a startup focused on renewable energy solutions. By keeping an open mind and staying receptive to new concepts, individuals can position themselves to capitalize on emerging trends and innovations, thereby enhancing their income potential.

In conclusion, the principles of wealth growth and investment are multifaceted, encompassing the notions of patience, entrepreneurship, and a proactive mindset. By embracing these principles and integrating them into one's financial strategy, individuals can set themselves on a path towards sustainable wealth creation and financial independence. In the subsequent sections of this chapter, we will delve deeper into specific investment strategies and entrepreneurial opportunities, providing practical insights and actionable guidance for achieving success in the realm of wealth growth and investment.

Once you begin investing and you've mastered the art of placing eggs in your basket of wealth, it's crucial to leave the money alone.

Your nest egg will continue to grow, especially if you come up with new ideas to generate money to save. Hard work pays off; you could sell **merchandise**, **eBooks, blogging**, **audio books,** or **some other form of e-learning**.

You could attend **a mastermind** or **brainstorming to gain more new ideas for cash generation.** You'll find favorable breaks by looking for them. As it grows it will look increasingly attractive to you, and you might be tempted to shave little funds from the top.

It's so important to **reinvest dividends** so that you generate the maximum amount of **compound interest.** The more you "mess" with your holdings, the less they will grow.

Possess the mental toughness that it requires to **keep growing wealth without spending to satisfy instant gratification**. Your mental strength will ultimately determine your **financial destiny.** No matter how much you make, you'll have to have **the discipline to spend less than you earn,** or you will never **gain financial independence.** You can easily create a lifestyle that exceeds your expenses, even if you are a millionaire.

Chapter 15: Pursuing High Returns through Diversified Investments.

In this pivotal chapter, we will embark on a journey to explore the strategies and principles behind pursuing high returns through diversified investments. We will begin by comparing the returns of traditional savings accounts with other high-yield investment options, shedding light on the potential for substantial growth through strategic financial decisions. Additionally, we will delve into the concept of equity as a powerful form of ownership in a company, unraveling the potential for profits and the associated risks. Finally, we will differentiate between individual stock investments, equity funds, and private equity investments, providing a comprehensive understanding of the diverse avenues for pursuing high returns.

Comparing Returns: Traditional Savings Accounts vs. High-Yield Investment Options

Traditional savings accounts have long been a popular choice for individuals seeking a secure repository for their funds. However, in today's dynamic financial landscape, the allure of high-yield investment options cannot be overlooked. By comparing the returns of traditional savings accounts with alternative investment avenues such as stocks, bonds, and mutual funds, individuals can gain insight into the potential for accelerated wealth growth. For instance, while a savings account may offer modest interest rates, savvy investors may opt to allocate a portion of their capital to diverse investment vehicles, thereby harnessing the power of compounding returns and market appreciation.

Strategies for Pursuing Higher Returns through Diversified Investment Portfolios:

Diversification lies at the heart of pursuing higher returns while mitigating risk. By constructing a well-balanced investment portfolio comprising a variety of assets such as stocks, bonds, real estate, and commodities, individuals can spread their risk and capitalize on diverse market conditions. For example, a prudent investor may allocate a portion of their portfolio to blue-chip stocks known for stability, while also embracing growth stocks with the potential for substantial returns. Through strategic asset allocation and periodic portfolio rebalancing, investors can optimize their chances of achieving attractive returns while safeguarding against undue volatility.

Equity Investing: Unveiling the Potential for Profits and Risks
The concept of equity, or ownership in a company, represents a compelling avenue for pursuing high returns in the realm of investments. By acquiring shares of a publicly traded company, individuals become partial owners, thereby gaining exposure to the company's performance and profitability. However, it's crucial to recognize the associated risks, including market volatility and the potential for financial loss. For instance, an individual investing in technology stocks may witness significant returns during bullish market conditions but must also brace for the impact of market downturns on their investment value.

Understanding Individual Stocks, Equity Funds, and Private Equity Investments:
In the landscape of equity investing, individuals are presented with a spectrum of options, each with its unique characteristics and considerations. Individual stock investments entail purchasing shares of a specific company, offering direct exposure to the company's performance. On the other hand, equity funds such as mutual funds and exchange-traded funds (ETFs) pool investors' resources to invest in a diversified portfolio of stocks, providing instant diversification and professional management. Furthermore, private equity investments cater to accredited investors and institutions, offering the opportunity to invest in private companies or participate in corporate buyouts, albeit with heightened complexity and illiquidity considerations.

In conclusion, the pursuit of high returns through diversified investments demands a nuanced understanding of risk, reward, and the dynamic interplay of financial markets. By embracing a diversified investment approach, individuals can position themselves to capitalize on lucrative opportunities while safeguarding against potential.

You can retire as a millionaire; it's possible if that's your goal. It doesn't require a great deal of money to invest in raising the funds to $1 million or some other profitable goals.

Remember that investing doesn' t have to be complicated and mysterious. Believing that you must invest in complicated matters that you don' t truly understand is a sure way to lose your wealth. There are more **practical ways to invest-aim for what you know while seeking to understand more.**

Your investments are mainly going to reflect where you are in life. There is no "best investment" that is a one size fits all.

Decide whether it' s more important to you to **increase the amount of money you hav**e or **preserve your savings**. As a person with **profitable goals**, you' re likely in a **wealth building stage** or a **wealth preservation stage**.

Chapter 16: Types of Fixed-Income Instruments

In this enlightening chapter, we will delve into the diverse universe of fixed-income instruments, shedding light on the intricacies of certificates of deposit, treasury bonds, preferred stock with stated dividend rates, and other notable vehicles. By providing concrete examples of fixed-income investments and their potential returns over time, we aim to offer readers a comprehensive understanding of these instruments' role in a well-rounded investment portfolio. Furthermore, we will meticulously analyze the suitability of fixed-income instruments for different investment objectives and risk profiles, empowering individuals to make informed decisions aligned with their financial aspirations.

Exploring Various Types of Fixed-Income Instruments:

Fixed-income instruments encompass a broad array of investment options, each presenting unique features and income-generating potential. From certificates of deposit (CDs) offering a guaranteed interest rate for a specified term to treasury bonds issued by the government and preferred stock with stated dividend rates, the landscape of fixed-income investments is rich with possibilities. For instance, treasury bonds, considered a benchmark for risk-free assets, provide regular interest payments and the assurance of principal repayment upon maturity, making them an attractive choice for risk-averse investors seeking stable income streams.

Illustrative Examples of Fixed-Income Investments and Their Potential Returns:

To elucidate the tangible benefits of fixed-income instruments, let's consider an individual who invests in a 5-year certificate of deposit with a competitive interest rate. Over the investment horizon, the individual receives periodic interest payments, culminating in the return of the initial investment upon maturity. Similarly, an investor who allocates funds to treasury bonds benefits from predictable coupon payments and the reassurance of the government's creditworthiness. By analyzing historical data and prevailing market conditions, investors can gauge the potential returns offered by fixed-income instruments, thus informing their investment decisions.

<u>Analyzing Suitability for Different Investment Objectives and Risk Profiles:</u>
The suitability of fixed-income instruments hinges on investors' unique objectives, risk tolerance, and time horizons. For conservative investors aiming to preserve capital and generate predictable income, fixed-income instruments serve as a cornerstone of a balanced portfolio. Conversely, investors pursuing aggressive growth strategies may allocate a smaller portion of their portfolio to fixed-income instruments, recognizing their role in hedging against market volatility and diversifying risk. Furthermore, individuals nearing retirement may prioritize fixed-income investments to secure a reliable income stream and shield their savings from market upheavals.

In conclusion, the realm of fixed-income instruments presents a mosaic of opportunities for income generation and risk management, catering to a spectrum of investor preferences and financial goals. By comprehensively understanding the nuances of certificates of deposit, treasury bonds, preferred stock, and other fixed-income instruments, individuals can craft investment strategies that align with their aspirations and pave the way for sustained financial well-being. In subsequent chapters, we will further explore the dynamics of fixed-income securities, debt instruments, and the pivotal role they play in shaping resilient and diversified investment portfolios.

Also, because you're reading a **<u>beginner's guide</u>**, it's not safe to assume that you're young. You may be in your 50s or 60s, and you need your investments to show that hard work pays off.

<u>Inflation will undoubtedly decrease the dollar's spending power.</u>

Choose investment vehicles that will at least allow you to beat inflation. Simply keeping your money in an account with no income-generating advantage could be equated to stuffing money in your mattress or the ground.

Experts will tell you to continue to find practical ways to gain income, whether that is **<u>blogging</u>**, **<u>hosting your radio programs</u>** or **<u>podcast-hard work pays no matter where your talents lie.</u>** There's no shame in getting **<u>the wisdom of experts involved in the planning of your financial future</u>**, plus they can give you proof of their methods of work.

Pulling money out of your mattress in 15 years will ultimately yield you less money than you started with. Inflation is proof of this.

Chapter 17: Attaining Financial Goals

In this transformative chapter, we will embark on a journey to illuminate the possibilities of achieving financial milestones, including the compelling prospect of retiring as a millionaire through disciplined investment and astute financial management. By delving into the attainability of financial goals through disciplined investing, we seek to empower readers to chart a course toward financial prosperity with confidence and clarity. Additionally, we will advocate for a simpler and more straightforward approach to investing, demystifying the complexities and fostering a mindset of purposeful wealth accumulation.

The Promise of Retiring as a Millionaire: A Testament to Disciplined Investment and Financial Management

Retiring as a millionaire stands as a tangible testament to the power of disciplined investment, prudent financial management, and unwavering resolve. By consistently allocating a portion of earnings to diverse investment vehicles and embracing a long-term perspective, individuals can set themselves on a trajectory toward realizing this compelling aspiration. For instance, envision an individual who diligently contributes to a retirement account, leveraging tax-advantaged investment options such as 401(k) plans and individual retirement accounts (IRAs). Over time, the compounding effect of regular contributions and strategic asset allocation can culminate in a substantial retirement nest egg, providing financial freedom and security in the golden years.

Attainability of Financial Goals through Disciplined Investing: Nurturing the Seeds of Prosperity:

The attainability of financial goals hinges on the steadfast commitment to disciplined investing, where each contribution serves as a seed nurturing the prospect of prosperity. Whether the goal involves purchasing a home, funding a child's education, or securing a comfortable retirement, the principles of disciplined investing remain constant. By setting clear objectives, formulating a well-defined investment strategy, and adhering to a consistent savings regimen, individuals can inch closer to the realization of their financial ambitions. Through a combination of diligence, patience, and informed decision-making, even the loftiest of financial goals can transition from aspiration to achievement.

Embracing Simplicity in Investing: Unveiling the Power of Clarity and Purpose:

In an era marked by complexity and information overload, there is profound merit in advocating for a simpler and more straightforward approach to investing. By distilling investment principles into clear, actionable steps and fostering a mindset of purposeful wealth accumulation, individuals can navigate the labyrinth of financial markets with confidence and conviction. This may involve embracing low-cost index funds for broad market exposure, prioritizing long-term asset allocation over short-term speculation, and minimizing the influence of market noise on investment decisions. Through simplicity, clarity, and a resolute focus on long-term objectives, individuals can harness the power of compounding returns and inch closer to their financial aspirations.

In conclusion, the journey toward attaining financial goals is imbued with promise, potential, and the prospect of transformative wealth creation. By championing disciplined investing, nurturing a vision of retiring as a millionaire, and embracing the virtues of simplicity in investing, individuals can pave a definitive path toward realizing their financial aspirations. In the subsequent chapters, we will unravel actionable strategies, investment frameworks, and wealth-building principles, further illuminating the road to financial fulfillment and prosperity.

If you' re **beginning your wealth creation journey**, remember that it is a journey, and you must be relentless. Think of how much you really spend on entertainment and other goodies; then think about how much money you can earn instead.

When you spend money as a consumer, it' s gone forever when it could have been working for you, **generating interest.**

Chapter 18: Wealth Building and Preservation

In this pivotal chapter, we will navigate the dynamic interplay between wealth building and wealth preservation, acknowledging the distinct stages in life where these pursuits take precedence. By differentiating between these stages and their implications for financial strategies, we aim to provide a comprehensive framework for individuals seeking to cultivate and safeguard their financial well-being. Furthermore, we will address the diverse age range of individuals seeking financial guidance, recognizing the intrinsic link between hard work, prudent investments, and the realization of long-cherished aspirations.

Understanding the Dynamics of Wealth Building and Preservation:
Wealth building and preservation represent two pivotal stages in the financial journey, each characterized by unique priorities, risks, and opportunities. The wealth building stage typically encompasses the formative years of one's career, marked by a focus on income generation, strategic investment in growth-oriented assets, and the pursuit of

long-term financial aspirations. In contrast, the wealth preservation stage unfolds as individuals approach retirement or seek to safeguard the fruits of their labor, emphasizing the need for stable income streams, capital protection, and prudent risk management. By discerning the distinct nuances of these stages, individuals can tailor their financial strategies to align with their evolving needs and aspirations.

<u>Catering to a Diverse Age Range: The Universal Need for Financial Guidance:</u>
The pursuit of financial well-being knows no bounds of age or circumstance, encompassing a diverse range of individuals seeking to chart a course toward prosperity. From young professionals embarking on their careers to seasoned veterans approaching retirement, the need for sound financial guidance remains a constant. For instance, a recent college graduate may prioritize aggressive wealth building strategies, seeking to capitalize on the power of compounding returns and long-term investment growth. Conversely, a pre-retiree may pivot towards wealth preservation, emphasizing the stability of income-generating assets and the preservation of accumulated wealth. By recognizing the diverse age range of individuals seeking financial empowerment, advisors and mentors can tailor their guidance to address the unique needs and aspirations of each demographic.

<u>Investments as Testaments to Hard Work and Payoff:</u>
The essence of investments lies in serving as testaments to hard work, dedication, and the unwavering pursuit of financial freedom. Whether it's allocating resources to an education fund for a child's future, constructing a diversified portfolio to fund entrepreneurial endeavors, or securing a comfortable retirement through prudent financial planning, investments reflect the culmination of effort and the anticipation of meaningful payoff. Each contribution to an investment vehicle represents a tangible step towards realizing cherished aspirations and fostering a legacy of prosperity. By infusing investments with purpose and intention, individuals can channel their hard-earned resources into vehicles that align with their vision for the future, thus setting the stage for enduring financial fulfillment.

In conclusion, the equilibrium between wealth building and preservation stands as a testament to the dynamic evolution of financial aspirations and the intrinsic link between hard work, prudent investments, and enduring payoff. By comprehensively understanding the distinct stages of wealth cultivation, recognizing the universal need for financial guidance across diverse age ranges, and infusing investments with purpose, individuals can sculpt a path toward sustained financial well-being, resilience, and enduring legacy. Subsequent chapters will delve deeper into actionable strategies, investment frameworks, and wealth-building principles, further illuminating the road to financial fulfillment and prosperity across life's diverse stages.

Think you have no money to invest? Do you have a hobby or other form of entertainment you regularly spend money on? **Create a pool to invest in by living off 90% of your income and saving 10% to invest**.

There are many new ideas emerging like **savings challenges to make way for investing to be possible.** No matter how small the amount you must invest may be, there are some investment vehicles you can use such as **fractional shares.**

By following the basic principles of achievement laid out here, you will certainly retire with a **healthy nest egg**. **Continue furthering your education through e-learning, eBooks, radio programs, audio books, attend at a mastermind, or sell merchandise.** You may find that forex trading is for you, or you may be clever enough to make gains from foreign exchange.

Keyword list

- Keyword #Used
- economic depression how to make money after economic depression.
- principles of achievement
- cryptocurrency
- favorable breaks
- foreign exchange
- profitable goals
- radio programs
- sell merchandise.
- brainstorming
- practical ways
- hard work pays.
- opportunities
- forex trading
- entertainment
- audio books
- mastermind
- e-learning
- new ideas
- education
- sponsors
- blogging, experts, eBooks proof